I0423223

ReBaselining America

Setting a foundation of liberty for the next 200 years

By

Tom Spence

Tom Spence

ISBN **978-1461074779**

Dedication

To those who engineered this great republic and understood with every breath the reality of Benjamin Franklin's words when he stated:

We must all hang together, or assuredly we shall all hang separately.

May we be inspired to such unified boldness and patriotism today!

Tom Spence

THE MAN IN THE ARENA

*It is not the critic who counts; not the man who points
out how the strong man stumbles, or where the doer
of deeds could have done them better. The credit
belongs to the man who is actually in the arena,
whose face is marred by dust and sweat and blood;
who strives valiantly; who errs, who comes short
again and again, because there is no effort without
error and shortcoming; but who does actually strive
to do the deeds; who knows great enthusiasms, the
great devotions; who spends himself in a worthy
cause; who at the best knows in the end the triumph
of high achievement, and who at the worst, if he fails,
at least fails while daring greatly, so that his place
shall never be with those cold and timid souls who
neither know victory nor defeat.*

Theodore Roosevelt

Excerpt from the speech
"Citizenship In A Republic",

Delivered at the Sorbonne, in Paris,
France on 23 April, 1910

Contents

Tom Spence

I cannot live without books.

Thomas Jefferson

Prologue

Oh but to have been in the company of our Founding Fathers in the decade that followed our independence from Great Britain; what a time that would have been. Never before in the history of this planet has humankind attempted something so daring on such a scale with such synergy as was the genesis of this nation.

Every breath and every drop of sweat and blood permeated the air with the realization of liberty, justice, responsibility, service, and love of one's fellow man. Power was dissected and reassembled, not for efficiency, but for providing no purchase for tyranny or corruption in a single man or government entity.

This Grand Experiment in the democratic republic we call the United States of America was a machine with many cogs and wheels which the designers knew would only work well with the oil of statesmanship and selflessness.

Today we ask, "Is it over?"

We wonder if the golden age of our republic is complete. We wonder if we will join the ranks of the quasi-liberated and know only a future decided by choices between the lesser of the evils presented. Will we join the ranks of other nations that were once great for other accomplishments and assume our status of only being able to look rearward to see our national glory?

Is it over?

Are we the generation that at last fails to preserve the blessings of liberty for our posterity?

We must agree to answer this question with a definitive **NO!**

We know that saying "no" also means paying a price. We may not pay the price in blood as our forefathers did, but we will pay in time, money, service, and a call to serve country and countryman above self.

We know that saying "no" also means that this is about more than changing our government. It is about changing ourselves and living with honor, courage, commitment, and love.

If you are ready to be a part of preserving the blessings of liberty not only for ourselves, but especially for our posterity, then read this book. It is not a blueprint for a new America. Such a moment in time has passed. Our Founding Fathers knew that opportunity would never come again.

The blueprint of the Founding Fathers is sound, but we have had cracks in the foundation of government and individual character in this nation. To address one without the other is but to engage in chasing our tail without stopping to check our progress.

*These are the times that try men's
souls.*

Thomas Paine

Make no mistake; the years ahead will be trying
times. We are faced with a choice. Will we as a
nation shrink away from the challenges set before us
or will we embrace them as a divine destiny entrusted
to us by the Creator himself? The time to choose is
upon us. Are we ready for the challenges of liberty
in this new century and new millennium? I pray that
we are.

*See, I have refined you, though not
as silver;
I have tested you in the furnace of
affliction.*

Isaiah 48:10

Tom Spence

We in America do not have government by the majority. We have government by the majority who participate.

Thomas Jefferson

Once Upon a Time

It seems that all good stories begin once upon a time. That's not quite true. Once upon a time conveys that such a time no longer exists. What an exciting time it must have been in the late eighteenth century. Daring men were forming a new country. They did not know if they would be writing words for their posterity or a confession by which their British rulers may dispense with the formality of a trial and go straight for the noose. They prayed for the former.

This was a time when service to others, personal sacrifice, and a love of one's fellow man abounded. Such considerations were surely woven into the very fabric of our republic. Such precepts anchored the Constitution that would follow after more than a decade of trial and error in this grand experiment of self government.

But that was once upon a time. Partisan politics, self serving public servants, and a general sense of apathy on one end and extremism on the other rule today's political climate. Our most astonishing form of government was paid for with the blood of patriots.

Is there a way to get back to the principles that formed the genesis of our beloved nation without once again paying the price in blood? Is there a way to regenerate the love of country that compelled men to live such sacrificial lives for the benefit of those who would follow?

Is there a way to ReBaseline America?

11

Tom Spence

Let's begin by looking at a document that few Americans have actually read, the Declaration of Independence. This one is provided with original spelling and syntax.

Declaration of Independence

(Adopted by Congress on July 4, 1776)

The Unanimous Declaration of the Thirteen United States of America

When, in the course of human events, it becomes necessary for one people to dissolve the political bands which have connected them with another, and to assume among the powers of the earth, the separate and equal station to which the laws of nature and of nature's God entitle them, a decent respect to the opinions of mankind requires that they should declare the causes which impel them to the separation.

We hold these truths to be self-evident, that all men are created equal, that they are endowed by their Creator with certain unalienable rights, that among these are life, liberty and the pursuit of happiness. That to secure these rights, governments are

12

instituted among men, deriving their just powers from the consent of the governed. That whenever any form of government becomes destructive to these ends, it is the right of the people to alter or to abolish it, and to institute new government, laying its foundation on such principles and organizing its powers in such form, as to them shall seem most likely to effect their safety and happiness. Prudence, indeed, will dictate that governments long established should not be changed for light and transient causes; and accordingly all experience hath shown that mankind are more disposed to suffer, while evils are sufferable, than to right themselves by abolishing the forms to which they are accustomed. But when a long train of abuses and usurpations, pursuing invariably the same object evinces a design to reduce them under absolute despotism, it is their right, it is their duty, to throw off such government, and to provide new guards for their future security. --Such has been the patient sufferance of these colonies; and such is now the necessity which constrains them to alter their former systems of government. The history of the present King of Great Britain is a history of repeated injuries and usurpations, all having in direct object the establishment of an absolute tyranny over these states. To prove this, let facts be submitted to a candid world.

He has refused his assent to laws, the most wholesome and necessary for the public good.

Tom Spence

He has forbidden his governors to pass laws of immediate and pressing importance, unless suspended in their operation till his assent should be obtained; and when so suspended, he has utterly neglected to attend to them.

He has refused to pass other laws for the accommodation of large districts of people, unless those people would relinquish the right of representation in the legislature, a right inestimable to them and formidable to tyrants only.

He has called together legislative bodies at places unusual, uncomfortable, and distant from the depository of their public records, for the sole purpose of fatiguing them into compliance with his measures.

He has dissolved representative houses repeatedly, for opposing with manly firmness his invasions on the rights of the people.

He has refused for a long time, after such dissolutions, to cause others to be elected; whereby the legislative powers, incapable of annihilation, have returned to the people at large for their exercise; the state remaining in the meantime exposed to all the dangers of invasion from without, and convulsions within.

He has endeavored to prevent the population of these states; for that purpose obstructing the laws for naturalization of foreigners; refusing to pass others to encourage their migration hither, and raising the conditions of new appropriations of lands.

He has obstructed the administration of justice, by refusing his assent to laws for establishing judiciary powers.

He has made judges dependent on his will alone, for the tenure of their offices, and the amount and payment of their salaries.

He has erected a multitude of new offices, and sent hither swarms of officers to harass our people, and eat out their substance.

He has kept among us, in times of peace, standing armies without the consent of our legislature.

He has affected to render the military independent of and superior to civil power.

He has combined with others to subject us to a jurisdiction foreign to our constitution, and unacknowledged by our laws; giving his assent to their acts of pretended legislation:

For quartering large bodies of armed troops among us:

For protecting them, by mock trial, from punishment for any murders which they should commit on the inhabitants of these states:

For cutting off our trade with all parts of the world:

For imposing taxes on us without our consent:

For depriving us in many cases, of the benefits of trial by jury:

For transporting us beyond seas to be tried for pretended offenses:

For abolishing the free system of English laws in a neighboring province, establishing therein an arbitrary government, and enlarging its boundaries so as to render it at once an example and fit instrument for introducing the same absolute rule in these colonies:

For taking away our charters, abolishing our most valuable laws, and altering fundamentally the forms of our governments:

For suspending our own legislatures, and declaring themselves invested with power to legislate for us in all cases whatsoever.

He has abdicated government here, by declaring us out of his protection and waging war against us.

He has plundered our seas, ravaged our coasts, burned our towns, and destroyed the lives of our people.

He is at this time transporting large armies of foreign mercenaries to complete the works of death, desolation and tyranny, already begun with circumstances of cruelty and perfidy scarcely paralleled in the most barbarous ages, and totally unworthy the head of a civilized nation.

He has constrained our fellow citizens taken captive on the high seas to bear arms against their country, to become the executioners of their friends and brethren, or to fall themselves by their hands.

He has excited domestic insurrections amongst us, and has endeavored to bring on the inhabitants of our frontiers, the merciless Indian savages, whose known rule of warfare, is undistinguished destruction of all ages, sexes and conditions.

In every stage of these oppressions we have petitioned for redress in the most humble terms: our repeated petitions have been answered only by repeated injury. A prince, whose character is thus marked by every act which may define a tyrant, is unfit to be the ruler of a free people.

Nor have we been wanting in attention to our British brethren. We have warned them from time to time of attempts by their legislature to extend an unwarrantable jurisdiction over us. We have reminded them of the circumstances of our emigration and settlement here. We have appealed to their native justice and magnanimity, and we have conjured them by the ties of our common kindred to disavow these usurpations, which, would inevitably interrupt our connections and correspondence. They too have been deaf to the voice of justice and of consanguinity. We must, therefore, acquiesce in the necessity, which denounces our separation, and hold them, as we hold the rest of mankind, enemies in war, in peace friends.

We, therefore, the representatives of the United States of America, in General Congress, assembled, appealing to the Supreme Judge of the world for the rectitude of our intentions, do, in the name, and by the authority of the good people of these colonies, solemnly publish and declare, that these united colonies are, and of right ought to be free and independent states; that they are absolved from all allegiance to the British Crown, and that all political connection between them and the state of Great Britain, is and ought to be totally dissolved; and that as free and independent states, they have full power to levy war, conclude peace, contract alliances, establish commerce, and to do all other acts and things which independent states may of right do. And for the support of this declaration, with a firm reliance on the protection of Divine Providence, we mutually pledge to each other our lives, our fortunes and our sacred honor.

New Hampshire: Josiah Bartlett, William Whipple, Matthew Thornton

Massachusetts: John Hancock, Samual Adams, John Adams, Robert Treat Paine, Elbridge Gerry

Rhode Island: Stephen Hopkins, William Ellery

Connecticut: Roger Sherman, Samuel Huntington, William Williams, Oliver Wolcott

New York: William Floyd, Philip Livingston, Francis Lewis, Lewis Morris

New Jersey: Richard Stockton, John Witherspoon, Francis Hopkinson, John Hart, Abraham Clark

Pennsylvania: Robert Morris, Benjamin Rush, Benjamin Franklin, John Morton, George Clymer, James Smith, George Taylor, James Wilson, George Ross

Delaware: Caesar Rodney, George Read, Thomas McKean

Maryland: Samuel Chase, William Paca, Thomas Stone, Charles Carroll of Carrollton

Virginia: George Wythe, Richard Henry Lee, Thomas Jefferson, Benjamin Harrison, Thomas Nelson, Jr., Francis Lightfoot Lee, Carter Braxton

North Carolina: William Hooper, Joseph Hewes, John Penn

South Carolina: Edward Rutledge, Thomas Heyward, Jr., Thomas Lynch, Jr., Arthur Middleton

Georgia: Button Gwinnett, Lyman Hall, George Walton

Source: The Pennsylvania Packet, July 8, 1776

While much of this document appears to be personally directed to George III, we see many of the alleged infringements against the American colonials surfaced as rights in the Constitution and its first amendments that followed about eleven years later.

We in this country can never quite taste the struggle for freedom that our Founding Fathers knew. They believed that power must come from the people; but they had to wrestle such power from a monarch that was among the pioneers of world-wide force projection.

We in this age have lived with rights all of our lives. We did not have to earn them, fight for them, or do anything special other than by the grace of God be born in a country—or manage to migrate to a country—where these rights were there waiting upon us.

We cannot recreate 1776. Time has marched on. We must look at our present world and at our own values and then decide what we must do to put America back on course. We must look inward, upward, and then decide what to do to go forward.

What makes this treatise any different than a State of the Union address or the rebuttal of the opposition party?

It aims to work only on the foundation, not the superstructure of the implementing details. It seeks to challenge and sometimes provoke critical thinking alongside creativity. It purports to address what some may consider radical and resolve to reconcile these approaches with mainstream values.

This is not a plan to fix everything. It is a challenge to agree upon the base course for our nation and ask that we of this generation be willing to pay the price for what we value the most.

Tom Spence

Fear has its use but cowardice has none.

Mohandas Gandhi

Draft Dodgers

That seems to be a strange place to begin. We have
not used the draft since the Vietnam War. What does
that have to do with going forward?

After two hundred years of thriving as a republic,
President Jimmy Carter pardoned those who evaded
the draft for the Vietnam War. It was among his first
official acts as President of the United States. Its
purpose was to begin the healing process in a nation
divided by a conflict of dubious origins.

It was the right thing to do, but surely the wrong
time.

Some had answered the call when their number was
selected. Some volunteered for military service
trusting that their nation was certain of its course.
Others refused to be inducted and were convicted of a
crime and sentenced to punishment. Others left the
country.

We must salute three of the four groups that emerged
from this national event. Those who served as
inductees, those who volunteered and served, and
those who refused to go but paid the price demanded
by law. Each did what they thought was right.

The fourth group—the draft dodgers—practiced the
age old art of cowardice. They ran in the face of
danger. Many of these were fathers and sons who

were loved by their families--families who stood by them regardless of their choices.

To pardon—to forgive—was essential. We are a nation that is at its best when we are merciful and forgiving; however, we should have first pardoned those who would not be drafted and remained in this country to face the music. They broke the law, but they maintained their integrity. They did not serve in harm's way, but they were not afraid of living by the consequences of their decisions.

Consider what a different course this country might have navigated if our jails and prisons were full of young men who did not believe in the war and who were willing to accept the judgment of the courts. How much would the national debate have been truncated if there were no room for murderers, arsonists, and rapists in our prisons because they were full of honorable men?

To pardon those who fled this nation was to forgive when no repentance was sought. This parallels the grace of God, but we are still flawed humans who have a long way to go to practice such grace with the same precision and excellence.

Why is this important as we consider setting a new baseline for America?

We must never again act out of convenience when principles are involved. We must not rush to cover wounds that still have infection in them. We must not endorse or reward thinking or decisions that discard courage.

We cannot turn back the clock and pardon those who served their time in prison first; and then as others came home in repentance and submission to the legal authority of this nation, subsequently convict and then pardon them for their transgressions. We can set a course from this point forward that values both courage and compassion.

Let's begin a list with these two qualities as candidates to be among those that would govern our course for the future.

Courage

Compassion

Tom Spence

When you are winning a war almost everything that happens can be claimed to be right and wise.

Winston Churchill

Repeal the War Powers Act

War is an ugly thing, but not the ugliest of things. The decayed and degraded state of moral and patriotic feeling which thinks that nothing is worth war is much worse. The person who has nothing for which he is willing to fight, nothing which is more important than his own personal safety, is a miserable creature and has no chance of being free unless made and kept so by the exertions of better men than himself.

John Stuart Mill

The authority to declare war resides in Congress. Article I, Section 8 of the Constitution specifically grants this power to the Congress of the United States. For more than half a century, this authority has moved more and more to the executive branch.

The discussion on this issue began at the inception of our nation. The original verbiage was changed from *make war* to *declare war* so that the president could repel attacks and invasions. This simple change of syntax should have been sufficient for the ages. As Commander-in-Chief of the Armed Forces of the United States, the president should be able to take

27

actions necessary for the defense of our nation. The decision as to whether or not to engage in war, however, was firmly seated in the Congress of the United States.

This very diverse body of saints and sinners, the selfless and selfish, the stainless and the soiled best represent the national will. If such a body deems it essential to declare war upon another nation or entity, then this is as close to having the nation behind our military actions as we will get.

At that point, the congress turns the war over to the president with one condition—win! When this nation goes to war, it must go as a nation. It's not send troops this week and see if we can fund them next week. It's all in or all out.

Should the congress declare war and the president decide to give such an order only lip service, he should be impeached for treason.

This nation should not engage in warfare lightly, but when it does so by the declaration of Congress, may God have mercy on those whom we engage. When we part from this basic tenant, we become vulnerable to divisiveness on the home front. We hand our enemies the very weapon by which to dismantle our national will.

Following the Vietnam War, the War Powers Act was to have addressed this deviation from the Constitution by requiring the president to consult with and to obtain some level of concurrence from the legislature. This law was flawed from the onset. If presidents are willing to ignore the Constitution of the United States—which is the supreme law of the land; how much easier will it be for them to set aside some ordinary act of Congress?

Courts have wrestled with the question as to whether a resolution of Congress is the same as a declaration of war. They lean towards a *de facto* siding with what actually transpired as evidence of such a declaration. This is in and of itself insanity. For a declaration of war to have to be interpreted by the courts to see if it really is a declaration of war says to the people whom have granted the Congress the authority to declare war that this is no declaration at all.

A declaration of war must be unmistakably a Declaration of War. We insist on decisiveness in our military commanders. Those without it pay for such vacillation in American blood. Should we accept less from the body that sends these young men and women into harm's way? If we are not all in, then we must be all out.

Sitting on the fence of indecisiveness with regard to war not only gives us splinters in our collective butts; it permits cowardice at the top levels of government while demanding courage on the front lines.

It is time to repeal the War Powers Act and demand that Congress step up to the plate and declare war when it is necessary and impeach presidents who attempt to usurp any part of this power.

Let's add faithfulness to the list of qualities by which we draft our new baseline. Each branch must be faithful to the Constitution of the United States to execute their duties only within the authority granted them.

Faithfulness

Courage

Compassion

No Professional Politicians

Our Founding Fathers knew that power corrupts and that absolute power corrupts absolutely. They did not realize that addiction to power corrupts as much as having absolute power, perhaps more.

Have we not endured enough from self-serving politicians who remember those that elected them only when it is time for reelection?

> *The tree of liberty must be refreshed from time to time with the blood of patriots and tyrants.*

> Thomas Jefferson

The seats of Congress must also be refreshed with fresh blood much more frequently. This thought does not require the same level of sacrifice as Jefferson's but does remind us that a government of the people does not fare well with a Congress full of professional politicians.

So do we need term limits?

Yes!

Constitutional Amendments are almost impossible to bring to fruition.

We don't need them. We limit the terms of our government officials with the vote. We tell our senators, "You have six years to accomplish all you

31

can. Don't plan on running for a second term. We are already looking for your replacement."

To accomplish something this radical, people must once again become engaged in this process of self government. They can't show up at the polls and hope they recognize somebody's name. Name recognition results in reelection. Fresh blood in Congress means that people must do some work to know the candidates.

But what if someone does a really good job in their first term?

Tell them, "Well done!" If the eighth man in the batting order hits a grand slam, he doesn't get to bat in the ninth position as well. He took his at bat, hit a home run, gets his handshakes, and then goes to the dugout with the other players.

Two years in the House of Representatives seems like a short time. Perhaps, but I would contend not too short. Ask a Marine who has spent two years in Iraq or Afghanistan how long or short two years is.

As a commanding officer, staff officer, or program manager I found a very consistent pattern in the Marine Corps. You had thirty days to get to know your job. By the ninety day mark, you should be having a significant impact upon your command or your programs.

Two years is sufficient time to make history!

Here is an analogy used by almost every professional trainer.

Do you consider yourself a hard worker?

Do you give you best at work?

Do you always seem to have loose ends at the end of each day?

If you were leaving on vacation tomorrow, could you get everything done today?

The answer isn't always "yes", but most admit that they get four or five times as much done as they need to when they know they are getting on an airplane for Hawaii in twelve hours.

Why?

We triage better than we do on a normal day. The things that just take up our time get set aside and we focus on the important things and what we can do about them. Everything else shrinks in importance.

If our representatives know that this is their congressional career—not just the beginning—this is it; would they not be motivated to accomplish all they can in the time they have? Would they not set aside pettiness in favor of true statesmanship? Would the fact that elected office is not a career path weed out some of the self-serving candidates from the onset?

But would such an approach not give special interest groups the inside track on Washington politics?

Actually, representatives would have little time for lobbyists once they knew that in a few short years they would be back among the people they represented. The term *Washington Politics* would be an anachronism. Everyone would just be there on temporary duty and not nearly as interested in the flirtatious nature of special interest groups hoping to establish long term relationships with lawmakers. The return on investment of the special interest dollar goes down quickly when there is one hundred percent turnover in the greater part of the legislature every two years.

Terms such as ranking or senior senator would fade from the legislative lexicon. All would be freshmen. All would begin with equal footing.

So what are we trying to quantify here? What term can we apply?

Let's start with the word "genuine." People are actually engaged in this crazy process of self government. They want to be an actual part of the process, not just a vessel of ongoing complaints.

Let's also add "unselfishness" or "selflessness" to the list. Elected officials don't seek office to feather their own nests. They must truly, genuinely, desire to serve others. They must value others more highly than themselves and live out their public service accordingly.

So here is our updated list.

Genuineness

Unselfishness

Faithfulness

Courage

Compassion

Tom Spence

Every man, conducting himself as a good citizen, and being accountable to God alone for his religious opinions, ought to be protected in worshiping the Deity according to the dictates of his own conscience.

George Washington

Separation of Church and State

Some readers will put this book on the shelf or burn it after reading the first part of this chapter.

Why?

Because we must begin by saying that the United States has never been a Christian nation. We were not designed to be a Christian nation. Our Founding Fathers, despite what many proclaim with the certainty of the Gospel, were not all Christians.

Almost all believed in God. Many were ordained ministers. Prayer was a staple of their eighteenth century diet, but they did not embark upon a course to build a Christian nation.

Hold on now. The back cover of this book says that the author is an ordained minister of the Cumberland Presbyterian Church. How can a minister hold such a belief?

Because it is the truth and the truth will set you free!

Our Founding Fathers desired to establish and our Constitution provides for the free exercise of religion.

> *Congress shall make no law respecting an*
> *establishment of religion, or prohibiting*
> *the free exercise thereof; or abridging the*
> *freedom of speech, or of the press; or the*
> *right of the people peaceably to assemble,*

37

> *and to petition the Government for a*
> *redress of grievances.*

This is not an oversight. These men of faith, many among whom were Christians, decided that religion was an individual decision. They desired to establish and protect the right of each individual to worship as he or she saw fit. Their experience with religion was unfortunately as distasteful as their experience with the British Crown. They did not want the people of this new nation to have any religion shoved down their throats.

For many years Christianity blossomed in this nation. The Great Awakenings that paralleled the growth of this nation were based in Christianity, but the Constitution never changed. It protected all religions.

Today it seems that Christianity is being persecuted in every public venue. That may be true to some extent, but Christians as well as adherents of other faith groups must realize that this country was not established to recognize one faith group over another.

The Constitution was ordained and established to protect religion from government. It seems that somehow that has all been turned upside down and now government is being protected from religion. The problem for Christians is that it is we who are upside down.

We go to a rally to support the display of the Ten Commandments in a public building then drive home by people who are homeless, hungry, and seem to have no hope. It is the Christian who is called to do something about the homeless, hungry, and who better than the Christian to deliver a message of hope. It doesn't really matter if we could display the Decalogue in every court house, cat house, and outhouse in the nation; if we don't live the Christian life, we have just been decorating walls with religious memorabilia.

If we really want the United States of America to be a Christian nation, then those claiming to follow Jesus must live the Christian life, at the root of which is to love one another.

It is love, not law, that makes a community, a state, or a nation one which seeks to glorify God. If those who follow Jesus want Christianity to outrank all other religions, then we know what to do. We may not want to do it, but we know what to do. He who wants to be first must be last.

If we want a Christian nation, then we must be willing to serve others before serving our own desires. We must regard others more than we regard ourselves. We must love both neighbor and enemy. We must accept that our supreme law of the land protects all religions—even those that seem radical, off beat, or just downright strange—and stop seeking the law to do what love should have first compelled us to do.

Tom Spence

Let's add "love" to the list.

Love

Genuineness

Unselfishness

Faithfulness

Courage

Compassion

Rights and Entitlements

I begin this section with a simple but perhaps controversial statement. ***You don't have any rights!***

You think that I am crazy? That may be true, but I am sure of my facts. You don't have any rights. You were given rights by the blood of patriots.

Hold on there! Our Declaration of Independence said we had rights, didn't it?

> *We hold these truths to be self-evident,*
> *that all men are created equal, that they*
> *are endowed by their Creator with certain*
> *unalienable rights, that among these are*
> *life, liberty and the pursuit of happiness.*

Yes, it lists three, none of which made it into the Constitution. The rights that made it into the Constitution may have been somehow circuitously derived from these three, but not without the spilled blood of many to permit such a monumental document to be written, take effect, and survive to the present.

Whenever we think that we are entitled to something, we are on the verge of losing it. Or as Thomas Paine said, "*That which we obtain too easily, we esteem too lightly.*"

If we think that rights just happen, then we do not value them. If we think that because we want something or that a certain cause would make our

41

lives easier, we must proceed with a very deliberate speed and all due caution before declaring such a want to be a right.

Today we live in culture that thinks the world, or at least our nation, owes them an income, health care, and free wireless internet. Not too many years ago much of our population believed that the nation only owed them a job. Now the thinking is, "Forget the job; just send me the money."

It seems that we have lost the can-do, pioneer spirit that made this a great nation. In my capacity as pastor, I cannot count the number of times that I have worked with those having trouble paying their bills but who did not want to go to work. People have told me to my face that they worked hard to get their disability. They don't even seem taken back when I tell them that the taxes of hard working people have made that possible.

Paul, writing to a church he had established in Thessalonica, conveyed this simple axiom. *You don't work. You don't eat.* Yes, Christians still take care of older widows and orphans, but they do not enable laziness and an entitlement mentality.

A much more recent man of precise words offered this most applicable axiom.

> *"A democracy cannot exist as a permanent form of government. It can only exist until the voters discover that they can vote themselves largesse from the public treasury. From that*

moment on, the majority always votes for the candidates promising the most benefits from the public treasury with the result that a democracy always collapses over loose fiscal policy, always followed by a dictatorship. The average age of the world's greatest civilizations has been about 200 years. These nations have progressed through this sequence: From bondage to spiritual faith; From spiritual faith to great courage; From courage to liberty; From liberty to abundance; From abundance to selfishness; From selfishness to apathy; From apathy to dependence; From dependence back into bondage."

Ben Franklin

How do we in this country break the cycle of self-destructiveness in the life cycle of democratically based governments?

We must end the entitlement mentality.

Many years ago, every recruit at the Marine Corps Recruit Depot learned this definition of discipline. It was, of course, punctuated by "sir" on both ends.

Sir! Discipline is the instant willing obedience to orders, respect for authority, and self reliance. Sir!

We need a major dose of this philosophy in our homes and our schools.

Tom Spence

Parents tell their children to sit quietly, do their chores, wash their hands, or go to bed and they do so obediently. There should not be an option to call DHS or some other agency because parents are strict. We are not talking about physical or emotional abuse here. This is about obedience.

The child that acts up in class and is sent to the principal's office doesn't rate a call to his lawyer or union representative. He rates some sort of punishment, extra work, or suspension. The parents must accept that in 99.999% of the time, it was not the teacher's fault that the child had a foul mouth, started a fight, or exposed himself to the class. The child learned those qualities at home. Neither child nor parent is entitled to a fair and impartial hearing to determine if the child was justified in telling his teacher what she could do with her split infinitives.

The single case of abuse must not be allowed to destroy the effectiveness of teachers, employers, supervisors, pastors, commanders, and others in positions of authority.

We must return to a culture that cherishes our rights without projecting contempt for authority.

We must develop self reliance anew from youngest to oldest. The concept of picking one's self up by the bootstraps and getting on with life despite the hardships, failures, or seemingly insurmountable challenges must again become commonplace.

Working with inmates, I saw what was called a "victim stance" on a regular basis. Victim stance is a defense mechanism that always makes the person a victim of any situation. So many clients would say that they would take any sort of work once they got out just to stay out of prison, and then get fired at their prison job because another inmate received an easier assignment or preferable shift. When asked what happened to make them fly off the handle, they said, "I couldn't handle that." They said, "It's not fair that I had to work the same shift two days in a row."

We used signs in the therapeutic community for really tough cases. I had one made up with a big light bulb on it that said, "We'll leave the light on for you." The inmates had all heard the Motel 6 commercial many times. The wearer was required to pace around the perimeter of the cellblock and if anyone asked him why he was walking around with the sign, he must respond: "I'm picking out my cell for when I come back."

Normally when the inmate was really mad, I would spend some time with him and ask him what he thought about having a nineteen year old, zit faced kid, with three months experience in the fast food industry as his supervisor. The reality would eventually sink in that saying they would take a job flipping burgers and keeping the job were two different things that were miles apart.

Tom Spence

Being corrected, chewed out, and told when and where to be were foreign concepts for many inmates. If this affliction had only been present on the inside of prisons, it would not be the epidemic that it is. This entitlement mentality, this unwillingness to take hold of whatever job had been given and do one's best, has spread to every corner of this great nation.

Self reliance must be resurrected.

This does not begin with our government. It begins in our homes, continues into our schools and churches, and eventually overwhelms our government.

Self reliance does not do away with mercy. We still need to be compassionate and merciful, but we must realize that feeding the entitlement mentality is neither. Stephen Covey often used the expression, *Give a man a fish and feed him for the day. Teach him to fish and feed him for a lifetime.*

The government doesn't owe you a job.

The government doesn't owe you an income.

If you struggle to make ends meet, working more and spending less are viable options.

If you don't work, you don't eat.

So what do we add to our list of qualities now?

Let's go with "truth," "respect for authority," and "self reliance."

Truth

Respect for authority

Self reliance

Love

Genuineness

Unselfishness

Faithfulness

Courage

Compassion

Tom Spence

No taxes can be devised which are not more or less inconvenient and unpleasant.

George Washington

Taxes

We need taxes.

The loose confederation of states that was our government before 1787 tried governing without much in the way of taxes. Had the British attacked in force before the end of the century, we might be singing *God Save the Queen* in our schools and the term "tee time" might be phonetically confusing and have nothing to do with a golf date.

Fortunately, this country got its act together at the federal level and was able to provide for the common defense in those formative years.

We need taxes, but not nearly so many as we have in this present time and not in so many different forms. Is there anything that is not taxed? Our forefathers dumped tea in Boston Harbor because they thought the British taxed them unfairly. If those brave men could only see us now. They might embrace the British as benevolent masters. But we threw off the British yoke and proved to the world that we could tax ourselves far beyond what some tyrant overseas could even imagine.

We live in a far more complicated world today. Fees, surcharges, taxes, and other words for taxes are ubiquitous. How do we get back to something that is fair, effective, and provides a good return on the taxpayer's investment?

Let's begin with this one premise. Taxes for the wage earner or small business man should not require a lawyer, tax professional, or dedicated accountant to figure out. Taxes must be simple.

Simple tax procedures do not require every American to spend a hundred bucks on tax software or preparation service and another hundred bucks of our tax money to check these returns in the labyrinth of the Internal Revenue Service. Taxes must be simple.

Let's take one more leap here. Taxes must be reasonable. I didn't say fair; that's a tougher nut to crack. They must be reasonable. How do we know what is reasonable? We require an annual accounting to the American people.

Do you remember the Parable of the Talents? There are three servants entrusted with their master's money. The master leaves for a long time and finally one day returns. Each servant gives an account of what he did with what he was given.

Do you think that such an accounting is possible today?

Even with the technology of this age, it is impossible. Why? Because the authority to tax has been extended beyond Congress. Once again, this most basic congressional function has been so widely dispersed among agencies, that no one really knows who is doing what to whom and what anyone is getting in return.

This is going to be tough to rebaseline. It is going to take radical steps. It may require the willingness to start over from ground zero with something ever so basic as flat rate taxes for federal, state, and local appropriations. This would require every agency, township, and flagship to examine its budget more closely and not spend beyond its appropriation.

Perhaps starting over is not required, but the taxation of the American people must be simple and understandable. Let's add "simple" to our list.

Simple

Truth

Respect for authority

Self reliance

Love

Genuineness

Unselfishness

Faithfulness

Courage

Compassion

Tom Spence

Gain all you can, save all you can, and give all you can.

John Wesley

Stewardship

Isn't that a church term?

You should hear it mentioned in church but it should not be confined there. This is the question that every American must ask themselves if we are truly to be a great nation. You have heard the question before. *What did you do with what I gave you?*

What will we do with the talents, gifts, money, knowledge, skills, abilities, resources, and influence with which we are blessed? Can we think beyond ourselves and also look out for our posterity?

This country is currently on track to be the world's ultimate consumer and most pitiful contributor. We use our time and resources to satisfy ourselves, but what are we leaving for future generations?

Is this about going green?

Yes and no. It is about understanding that we do not own this earth. The earth is entrusted to us. One hundred years from now there will be a completely different set of people on this solar orbiter. What will we leave them? What will be our legacy?

Stewardship must work both from the top down and the bottom up. Government must ask the question every time it appropriates funds or releases resources for commercial consumption. Over the past few decades, government has dabbled in stewardship and conservation. Wetlands that were used for

53

commercial or residential purposes had to be restored elsewhere. Trees that were harvested must be replaced with new growth. If you spilled toxic material, you can't just walk away; you must clean it up.

The problem is that when it takes law or regulation to enforce this way of life, that in itself tells us that stewardship is not a value which we have learned in our homes, schools, or churches. Conservation is only part of the equation. True stewards are proactive. They put the solution into effect before the problem is at a critical stage. Such thinking—such a lifestyle—values others more than self. This is more than selflessness. This is vision and leadership.

Regardless of your faith, read the Parable of the Talents. You will find it in Matthew 25:14-30. I have included it at the end of this book. Note that the first servant takes what was entrusted to him and goes at once to put his talent to work. This was not a spontaneous act. This first servant had prepared himself to be trusted with something valuable. When that day came, he knew exactly what to do.

We cannot change the course of this nation if our métier is moaning, groaning, and complaining. We must look upon what has been entrusted to us and ask, what can I do to make it better? We have many problems that we addressed poorly over the past half century that are now global issues. Clean air, clean water, deforestation, pollution in general, recycling, and other occasions where we were not very good stewards top the list. Instead of being the model of stewardship, we now come to the international stewardship conference as a two hundred year old rookie.

Christians believe that there will come a day when God will make all things new. Many would like to believe that day is coming very soon. Whether it comes in this decade or not for another millennia does not diminish the second thing that all Christians must realize. On or about that same time, we are all going to give an account as to what we did with what God gave us.

The renewal of all things by God does not lessen our responsibility to do good things with what we have been given this day.

Let's add "stewardship" to our list.

Stewardship

Simple

Truth

Respect for authority

Self reliance

Love

Tom Spence

Genuineness

Unselfishness

Faithfulness

Courage

Compassion

The Second Amendment

We cannot talk about setting the course for the future without adequately addressing the topic of guns, gun control, and the Constitution. The problem is that this discussion is not about fire arms at all. It is about the gestalt of the system of government we currently embrace. We cannot eliminate one part of the system without impacting the whole. The Second Amendment is the most controversial example of the wholeness of our system of government.

> *It is the nature of our republic, that our domestic tranquility is afloat on a sea that separates revolution and tyranny.*

> *The Biased Observer*

> 31 October 2000

Paradox of Power

I believe that gun control is fundamentally wrong.

Some readers will never make it to this paragraph after my last statement. That same group may believe that there is only a First Amendment in the Bill of Rights. There are ten and we can ignore none of them without eroding them all. If we want gun control, then we need to change the Constitution, not ignore it.

Tom Spence

The Second Amendment, like the others in the Bill of Rights, was written in the context of preventing tyranny. The founding fathers could not have envisioned a United States that grew to be the most powerful nation in the world. They did envision a country that preserved individual freedom for each successive generation. Their greatest perceived threat came from the government which they were creating--that it could become its own tyranny. Federal power was distributed among three branches of government and the several states; while rights were retained by the people. This is not a model for efficiency, but for preservation. Our model of government preserved individual rights that permitted its citizens to come to its defense against a foreign adversary or to overthrow its own tyranny. The Second Amendment is a paradox rooted in a country born out of revolution.

How can I defend this position when violent acts have crept into our schools, communities, and way of life? Every Officer of the United States takes an oath to support and defend the Constitution of the United States. That most fundamental document preserves the right of the people to keep and bear arms. It is used in the context of a well regulated militia, but the right is reserved to the people. Times and technology have changed the price we pay for this right. There was always a price, but now it appears to be much higher with the ubiquitous availability of semiautomatic and automatic weapons. The weapons themselves are not responsible for violent crime, but the lethality of today's weapons makes each act more atrocious. The real question before the American people--one that should have been placed bluntly before our presidential candidates--is whether or not we need to change the Second Amendment.

Some would argue that the NRA lobby is so strong that such a change is not possible. That may or may not have merit; however, they should not be the strongest lobby against change. The ACLU should be prime contender in such a brokered battle. The Second Amendment is the only place where the people themselves are empowered to preserve the security of a free state, and embodies the ultimate civil liberty. Some would argue that tyranny is no longer a threat and that the political power of our federal government has been kept in check. If this is your position, consider where the power to declare war resides--in the Congress. How then did we get involved in Korea, Vietnam, and the Gulf Wars? Those that would classify these as police actions only hide the truth in Orwellian terminology. These were wars. The executive branch usurped power from the legislative branch and the people of this country didn't have a say in the matter. The Congress later recovered part of its power via the War Powers Act, but how binding is such an ordinary law when ignoring the supreme law of the land created this situation. The founding fathers recognized that power abhors a vacuum. The Constitution is our foremost protection against the consolidation of power by a single group or individual.

But surely we must make an exception in the case of assault weapons--the founding fathers could not have envisioned such lethality in a domestic setting. No such exception can be made. The founding fathers could not have envisioned nationally syndicated newspapers either, but none of us would stand for regulating the USA Today, New York Times, or the Washington Post because they have become too influential. We tolerate unprofessional journalists because we know that the ethical ones are essential to a free state. Every individual freedom comes at a price.

To understand the paradox of the Second Amendment, we must look at the powers vested in Congress, specifically those enumerated in Article 1, Section 8. Congress is empowered to call forth the Militia to suppress Insurrections and repel Invasions. How can the same Constitution preserve the right of the individual to keep and bear arms while authorizing the Congress to suppress insurrection? The sanity in this is that it is the militia that is called forth to suppress insurrection, not the Armed Forces of the United States, which are addressed separately in this same section. It is the part time soldier--the militiaman-- that is vested with the responsibility to suppress an uprising or to join it if such a cause is to overthrow tyranny.

Gun control lobbyists have clouded the issue by focusing on handguns and appeasing the NRA that none of their proposed legislation will impact the rights of hunters. Hunters don't have any constitutional rights--the people do--regardless of whether they are outdoorsman or not. Both the NRA and their adversaries are evading the constitutional issue. The Second Amendment is designed to protect us against all enemies, including the accumulation of tyrannical power by our own government. This has created problems in that some extremist groups within our own country have become well armed. So long as these groups do not represent the values of our people, they will be a threat to our society. Should the individual liberties of this country be usurped by our government, such groups become the mainstream of liberty. It is the nature of our republic, that our domestic tranquility is afloat on a sea that separates revolution and tyranny.

I don't believe we are at either extreme today. Our biggest threat to our liberty is not that our government will be replaced via a Coup d'état, but that we will slowly erode the Constitution by ignoring it. If you don't believe this is possible, consider the fact that George Washington had to convince the founding fathers that he should not be king. Having just defeated a monarchy in forming our country, our founders considered establishing one of our own. Consider the illegal acts of two presidents, Nixon and Clinton. Nixon resigned for the good of the country. Clinton was impeached and evaded conviction not because he was innocent, but because he was popular and fought to retain power. Our Constitution recognized that power does indeed corrupt and it adequately distributed that power to avoid tyranny. The Constitution cannot contend with emotion, popularity, and impulse unless we honor it above capricious causes. We must aggressively fight crime and violence, especially in our schools. These solutions will come slowly and cannot be legislated. They must come from teaching the value of human life in our homes, schools, and churches.

The Constitution also provides a mechanism to deal with the needs of a changing society. The fifth article describes the constitutional process for changing our most fundamental document. It's a tough process. Obtaining a two-thirds majority in both houses of the Congress or three-fourths majority in a convention of the states requires the resolve of a nation. If we truly have a need to regulate guns in today's society, we need to amend the Constitution. Before we go down this road, we must carefully weigh what we are willing to give up in the way of liberty.

***

Consider where this discussion of rebaselining America began—with the Declaration of Independence.

> *Prudence, indeed, will dictate that governments long established should not be changed for light and transient causes; and accordingly all experience hath shown that mankind are more disposed to suffer, while evils are sufferable, than to right themselves by abolishing the forms to which they are accustomed. But when a long train of abuses and usurpations, pursuing invariably the same object evinces a design to reduce them under absolute despotism, it is their right, it is their duty, to throw off such government, and to provide new guards for their future security.*

The Second Amendment makes provision for the unimaginable. It makes provision for a time when a free press, the freedom to worship as we choose, and the sanctity of being secure in our homes is no longer secured by those whom comprise our government.

So what do we add to the list? Guns for everyone?

No. We add the word "integrity". Any change that we make must take into account the entire system of government, liberty, safeguards, responsibilities, and balance. As we seek to move forward, we must not do away with a part of our existing system as if it were an appendix until we know for sure how it will impact the rest of the system.

The word we will use for the systematic wholeness is "integrity".

Integrity

Stewardship

Simple

Truth

Respect for authority

Self reliance

Love

Genuineness

Unselfishness

Faithfulness

Courage

Compassion

Tom Spence

God: The most popular scapegoat for our sins.

Mark Twain

I know God will not give me anything I can't handle.
I just wish that He didn't trust me so much.

Mother Teresa

Some of God's greatest gifts are unanswered prayers.

Garth Brooks

There are two kinds of people: those who say to God,
"Thy will be done," and those to whom God says, "All
right, then, have it your way."

C.S. Lewis

God

Talk to men and women anywhere about the problems of this country and many will tell you that they exist because the government kicked God out of the schools, out of the courthouse, and out of just about every public place. There is a *theo-political* term for this sort of thinking.

Horsehockey!

But what about prayer in school? What about the display of the Ten Commandments in or around public buildings? What about the movement to take *In God we trust* off of our money?

God does not need the government's permission to enter the school house or the court house. The government cannot restrict the presence of the Almighty. God's Spirit hovered over the earth when it was but a formless entity and school houses and courthouses were millennia away.

The government, and we are talking mainly the courts, have ruled upon their interpretation of the First Amendment and have generally been of the consensus that the best way to protect the freedom of religion from the state is to permit no religion to claim privilege over those whom are in a public place. That may be a school, football field, courthouse, or other public place.

While most Christians have a hard time understanding this; most would also not want to give

Satan worshipers equal time for a school prayer. Most would not want to give this same group equal time and space to post something authored by the Father of lies next to the Decalogue. The courts—and I know that it is very popular to hate their decisions at this time in our nation's history—have done a fair job of protecting religious freedom by denying any faith to be the faith of the state.

So are we throwing in the towel on prayer in school and the Ten Commandments in the courthouse?

No. We need both but we don't need them to come into the school by an act of Congress. They need to come in as genuine acts of faith.

Take a moment. Close your eyes. Recite the Ten Commandments. How many did you get?

If you got all of them—in either of the two major versions—give yourself a pat on the back. That's long enough. Do you live them?

If you live in America, you probably don't even have to go beyond the part about *no other gods before Me.* What is it in this country that we don't worship? Money, sports icons, the newest pair of athletic shoes, entertainers, and even a show called American Idol tell us that we worship the things of this world.

But if we had the Ten Commandments posted everywhere, then we could live right.

No, then they would become like the Christian fish symbol on the back windshield of the car cutting people off in traffic and practicing digital communication with a single digit. The Ten Commandments would be everywhere but in the hearts and minds of the people.

But as we set upon a new course for America, should we not base our new laws on the Ten Commandments?

These are good guides to living for sure as the Law was intended to be from the beginning. Remember, though, that when left to their own devices, the Scribes and Pharisees took God's law and made it a burden to be born on the backs of men. They took a blessing and made it a burden. They embalmed the law that was meant to be internalized and lived out.

Would we not do the same? How would we enforce laws based upon the Ten Commandments anyway? Murder and stealing are pretty easy to identify and address, but how do we enforce the *thou shall not covet* legislation? Orwell wrote of the thought police. Would we commission an enforcement agency of heart and mind police?

Let's be very honest. God has not been kicked out of the schools or the courthouse or the football stadium. We just have not included him as the center piece of our lives.

We add God as an afterthought when he must be the *sine qua non*. We throw in an occasional *in the name of Jesus* in a time of crises, but hardly resemble people who are strangers in this world because we follow a man who said deny yourself every day, pick up your cross, and follow me.

We would prefer just to meet Jesus at his destination instead of following him through trials, suffering, and persecution.

God has not been evicted from the schools. We have used this lame excuse not to bring him to the very center of our lives. If the message of good news is not present in our schools it is because it does not live in our very being. We said the words, "Sure, I believe Jesus is the Son of God and died for me," but forgot that we were called to live in response to this wonderful gift of grace by spreading the good news, being a light for the world, and loving others more than ourselves.

For good news to be good news it really has to be good news. We treat the gospel of salvation like it was the farm and ranch report. "I'll say something if it comes up in conversation."

This is for the old people who are still reading at his point. By old people, I mean my age. What happens when you get a new picture of one of your grandkids? Do you keep it in your desk drawer and say I will break it out if someone comes by and specifically says, "Do you have any grandchildren and might you have a new photo close by?"

Of course not, you are showing off that grandbaby from birth to college graduation or enlistment in the Marine Corps. You break out your pictures for close friends, work associates, and people you just bump into at the post office. "There sure is a line to get stamps today *wannaseemygrandson*?" That picture is out and in front of the man you have known only for the thirty-six seconds in which you have been standing in line behind him.

Not so with the good news of salvation. We seem to be looking for that one exact moment in which we are to share with someone that we know for sure wants to hear about Jesus, or at least about going to church, or at least about be a pretty good person, or at least not being an axe murderer. We could testify that axe murderers are bad. Yeah, we could do that.

We are a nation of wimps when it comes to sharing our faith.

We might be in line at the post office. There are only two people in line. You have been praying occasionally that God would make this witnessing stuff straightforward for you. The man in front of you turns around and says, "I wish someone would tell me about God."

What do we do?

We silently ask God, "Please give me a sign. Is this the one?"

We are a nation of wimps when it comes to sharing our faith. How can we expect God to be in our schools and government buildings if we can't share what we believe on a one-to-one basis?

Our Founding Fathers knew that no government could survive—especially one conceived in liberty—without men and women of faith. They did not go so far as to legislate this country to be a Christian nation, but they enabled those commissioned by Christ to fulfill their mission as in no other nation in history.

We need God in the center of our nation. We don't get him there by an act of Congress. We make God the center of our nation by making him the center of our lives, of our families, of our churches, and of everything that we do. We live as the light of the world and the salt of the earth. When people see how we live and taste of our love, they should be compelled to ask, "Could this be anything but a Christian?"

Let's put God at the top of our list and keep him there, then let's begin this day to put him in the center of our lives.

God

Integrity

Stewardship

Simple

Truth

Respect for authority

Self reliance

Love

Genuineness

Unselfishness

Faithfulness

Courage

Compassion

Tom Spence

To the press alone, chequered as it is with abuses, the world is indebted for all the triumphs which have been gained by reason and humanity over error and oppression.

James Madison

Freedom of the Press

It seems that every appendage of the monster that claims to fall within the protection of the First Amendment is either viewed as too conservative, too liberal, or too commercially oriented. These observations surely have elements of truth, the lens of bias, and the potential for either synergy or controversy.

Controversy, acrimony, bitterness, vitriol, pandering, and showboating are all words that come to mind when we think of the free press these days. How do we get back to the press being the watchdog of government?

We must remember that to be a watchdog, you need a fierce bark and a few sharp teeth. When real danger lurks, you must stand your ground.

"Though all the winds of doctrine were let loose to play upon the earth, so Truth be in the field, we do injuriously by licensing and prohibiting to misdoubt her strength. Let her and Falsehood grapple, who ever knew Truth put to the worse in a free and open encounter?"

John Milton

Do we want a press that is less interested in profit and more in discovery and revelation of the truth? Turn off the talking heads. Do you think that one network or news organization is too liberal or too conservative or just avoids the real stories all around us? Turn them off.

The right to free speech and free press is not accompanied by a corresponding duty to listen. When people start turning off traditional media in favor of reliable alternative sources—including investigating for themselves; these media will once again begin to police themselves.

No change is needed in our Constitution with regard to the freedoms guaranteed by the First Amendment. What is needed is that every American value his or her time on this planet and turn off all of the talking heads.

Do we really need to hear why the problem wasn't fixed from forty different vantage points? No, we need to ignore the promises, excuses, accusations, and counter accusations and tell our government officials to get back to work solving problems instead of pointing fingers at each other. The message to the press is: *Don't bother me with filler. Until you can prove your value as a true watchdog of government, I'm turning you off.*

Every hour spent watching or listening to programs with five people trying to talk at once and a moderator badgering each one when they venture too close to cogent thought could be an hour spent working on a problem in your own community.

Our press needs to be the watchdog of government, but we need to keep this animal hungry. We don't feed him until he proves his worth. Likewise, an unwatched news network or a newspaper without subscribers loses advertising revenue quickly. It is the viewers and subscribers of the free press who have control over how effective our watchdog is.

If we feed him only because he is hungry, he will forget what it is like to be hungry.

Likewise, we all need to be hungry for the truth. Let's add "hunger for the truth" to our list.

God

Hunger for the Truth

Integrity

Stewardship

Simple

Truth

Respect for authority

Self reliance

Love

Genuineness

Tom Spence

Unselfishness

Faithfulness

Courage

Compassion

Equal Justice, Protection, and Opportunity

All persons born or naturalized in the United States, and subject to the jurisdiction thereof, are citizens of the United States and of the State wherein they reside. No State shall make or enforce any law which shall abridge the privileges or immunities of citizens of the United States; nor shall any State deprive any person of life, liberty, or property, without due process of law; nor deny to any person within its jurisdiction the equal protection of the laws.

From the 14th Amendment to the Constitution

The United States must once again be the land of opportunity. It must be a place where hard work and continued education transcend generations of poverty and ignorance. We should be a nation that seeks equal justice, equal protection, and equal opportunity not only under the law but by a spirit of justice and fairness that abides within every American.

That means that we need to abandon causes to make a group of people a special group with special rights. Among the popular examples in this line of thinking is that Congress should make no law which does not apply to them as it does to the population at large. There would be no special health care system, special retirement system, or unchecked expense system. To serve the people as direct representatives, these law makers must live as the people.

Among the sometimes less than popular examples in this line of thinking is that no one group would have special laws that apply to them unless there is overwhelming evidence to demand such legislation. Americans with disabilities might meet this threshold. Homosexuals do not. Members of a certain race or culture do not. Christian, Muslims, and Jews do not. Fat, bald, biased white people do not fit a special privilege category.

Hate crimes should not exist. If you torture, rape, kill, or otherwise do terrible things to a person; hate—malice aforethought—criminal intent is already an element of the crime. The crime does not become worse because the victim was black, gay, gray-haired, fat, or had poor taste in clothing and television shows. To truly have justice, fairness, and equality under the law, murdering anyone must be considered a terrible thing regardless of who the victim is. We must return to valuing life, valuing each other, and desist from dividing this nation into special rights groups.

To say the crime is mitigated or aggravated by the race, gender, sexual orientation, or sense of humor of the victim is to continue down a path that seeks to divide the nation for the good of the individual at the expense of all.

We have come to a point in modern society where a man or woman may vault past his or her past into financial, social, or political success. We no longer need to give one group a head start on another. Such continued practices create the entitlement mentality previously discussed. In today's world, all in this nation are equally advantaged and disadvantaged. No group needs a leg up on another for past wrongs, current trials, or presumed damages from something that might happen.

Yes, there are exceptions, but we must reverse the trend where exceptions are so numerous and self-serving as to supplant the norm.

For America to go forward we must do so as Americans. The melting pot must produce an alloy with all of the best characteristics of the contributing elements but be one metal.

Some will be angered by this philosophy, especially if their group has special rights, privileges, or other protected status that might be sacrificed. Make no mistake about it. This is a go/no go criterion. We all must be willing to sacrifice if we are to go forward together.

Mercy and compassion will dictate when and where a group may need special consideration. Lobbying for special status must be considered poison. One of the defense mechanisms that alcoholics and drug addicts frequently resort to in resisting treatment is called uniqueness. Yes, God made us all in his image and

79

all unique in the same stroke of creation, but the defense mechanism of uniqueness is something altogether different.

Uniqueness says that I am the individual to which the norms do not apply. *Yes, I know that for hundreds of thousands of other men and women, taking just one drink is one drink too many, but I am different. My problem was drinking hard liquor so I am sure that I will be fine with a couple of beers.*

Uniqueness in addicts is a defense mechanism used so the addict does not have to confront his disease. The addict continues to deny that he has a disease. Uniqueness in a system of laws, values, and ethics cripples a family, a community, and a nation. We cannot have equal justice or equal protection under the law when so many seek a privileged status in the law.

Consider words spoken clearly a half century ago. To some they bring promise and hope. To others they speak of promises unfulfilled. For us, they should speak to our hearts if we truly want to preserve what is good in the county for generations to come.

*In the long history of the world, only a few
generations have been granted the role of
defending freedom in its hour of maximum
danger. I do not shrink from this
responsibility – I welcome it. I do not believe
that any of us would exchange places with any
other people or any other generation. The
energy, the faith, the devotion which we bring
to this endeavor will light our country and all
who serve it – and the glow from that fire can
truly light the world.*

*And so, my fellow Americans: ask not what
your country can do for you – ask what you
can do for your country.*

*My fellow citizens of the world: ask not what
America will do for you, but what together we
can do for the freedom of man.*

*Finally, whether you are citizens of America
or citizens of the world, ask of us the same
high standards of strength and sacrifice which
we ask of you. With a good conscience our
only sure reward, with history the final judge
of our deeds, let us go forth to lead the land
we love, asking His blessing and His help, but
knowing that here on earth God's work must
truly be our own.*

John F. Kennedy

Inaugural Address 1961

For those who might contend that this will cripple not the nation but millions of individuals who need these special laws and privileges and status; I commend to you the reading of a book even shorter than this one penned in 1899 by Elbert Hubbard. It is *A Message to Garcia*. Here is a piece from the conclusion.

> *Have I put the matter too strongly? Possibly I have; but when all the world has gone a-slumming I wish to speak a word of sympathy for the man who succeeds - the man who, against great odds, has directed the efforts of others, and having succeeded, finds there's nothing in it: nothing but bare board and clothes. I have carried a dinner pail and worked for day's wages, and I have also been an employer of labor, and I know there is something to be said on both sides. There is no excellence,* per se, *in poverty; rags are no recommendation; and all employers are not rapacious and high-handed, any more than all poor men are virtuous. My heart goes out to the man who does his work when the "boss" is away, as well as when he is at home. And the man who, when given a letter for Garcia, quietly takes the missive, without asking any idiotic questions, and with no lurking intention of chucking it into the nearest sewer, or of doing aught else but deliver it, never gets "laid off" nor has to go on a strike for higher wages.*

Civilization is one long anxious search for just such individuals.

Anything such a man asks shall be granted. He is wanted in every city, town and village - in every office, shop, store and factory. The world cries out for such: he is needed and needed badly - the man who can "Carry a Message to Garcia."

We must decide in the next few years—a decade may be too long—to continue along the every man for himself or every group for itself; or decide that we will sacrifice our personal privileges for the good of all and the good of our great grandchildren.

Will we choose selfishness or sacrifice?

Tom Spence

The ultimate measure of a man is not where he stands in moments of comfort, but where he stands at times of challenge and controversy.

Martin Luther King, Jr.

The Next 200 Years

We can't control what the market will do tomorrow. We don't know the extent of nuclear danger from a crippled reactor. We don't know when the next big earthquake or massive hurricane will strike. We don't know the whereabouts of every person with evil in their hearts who are this very hour planning destruction upon the land of the free and the home of the brave. We don't know if the earth will be ten degrees warmer in fifty years or just continue on a rhythmic cycle that goes beyond our meteorological history.

The list of things that we don't know or can't control is substantial.

We have examined qualities that we can exert or influence by our personal actions. These qualities pursued with God in the center of our lives will surely give us a fighting chance to preserve the blessings of liberty for our posterity.

Hunger for the Truth, Integrity, Stewardship, Simple, Truth, Respect for authority, Self reliance, Love, Genuineness, Unselfishness, Faithfulness, Courage, and Compassion are all qualities that we can develop in ourselves and our children. Put God squarely in the center of this process and how can we fail?

Tom Spence

> *What, then, shall we say in response to these things? If God is for us, who can be against us?*

Romans 8:31

Fourteen prime considerations seem like a bunch, don't they?

Consider that an eighteen year old kid is put into culture shock the second he steps off the bus at Marine Corps boot camp. Thirteen weeks later he is healthier and has learned more information and more about himself than ever before. Among what he has learned are fourteen leadership traits.

They are justice, judgment, decisiveness, integrity, dependability, tact, initiative, enthusiasm, bearing, unselfishness, courage—both moral and physical, knowledge, loyalty, and endurance. If a young man under stress can learn these fourteen traits, cannot we not at least strive to engage fourteen qualities than may get our country back on track and rescue us from the abruptly short life expectancy of a democracy?

I pray that we can.

I believe that we can.

Provided for Additional Background

It is difficult to set a new course if you don't know the seas upon which you are sailing. It is difficult to repair a foundation, if you don't know where the existing one is solid or cracked. Likewise, a little history and insight into why some of the things are as they are is worth a few moments.

Two of these exposés follow a serious vein throughout; perhaps the third will provide sufficient levity to make the journey less taxing.

Tom Spence

*But, in a larger sense, we cannot dedicate—we
cannot consecrate—we cannot hallow—this ground.
The brave men, living and dead, who struggled here,
have consecrated it, far above our poor power to add
or detract. The world will little note, nor long
remember what we say here, but it can never forget
what they did here. It is for us the living, rather, to be
dedicated here to the unfinished work which they who
fought here have thus far so nobly advanced. It is
rather for us to be here dedicated to the great task
remaining before us—that from these honored dead
we take increased devotion to that cause for which
they gave the last full measure of devotion—that we
here highly resolve that these dead shall not have
died in vain—that this nation, under God, shall have
a new birth of freedom—and that government of the
people, by the people, for the people, shall not perish
from the earth.*

Abraham Lincoln

A Good Read

I re-read an old favorite of mine just because I picked
it up again. I guess you would call it a political
thriller, though some might not find it so exciting. It
doesn't have the high tech warfare you might find in a
Tom Clancy novel, but it is set forth in a time like our
own when the political situation is somewhat
tenuous. There has been significant battle and
bloodshed to this point, but the real struggle is more
Machiavellian in nature. I doubt that you will see
this one in movie form. Harrison Ford, Brad Pitt, and
Demi Moore are not knocking at the door for lead
roles. This work would just be too tough to cast.
While the power struggle remains the same, the cast
involved in that struggle changes too frequently to
accommodate Hollywood egos and budgets. This is
one of those classics where the struggle itself is much
greater than any single protagonist or villain. It has a
certain Shakespearean allure not only because of the
intricacies of the power struggle, but because like the
English Playwright's works, there is some question as
to whether or not this one has a single author.

A good work always has conflict. A great work
intricately ties in not only a struggle between good
and evil, but struggles among noble causes as well.
Quests for perfection, justice, or tranquility cause the
reader to yearn for the next line or next page with the

same or even greater anxiousness contained in a well spun mystery. Shared existential risk balanced against noble ideas such as protecting the welfare of others--even the liberty of another generation-- increases the drama of each successive word. You won't buy the Cliff's Notes for this one. The commentaries and reviews far exceed the length of the work itself. You will, however, remember a line or two from this one, whether you have read it or not. It begins, "We The People..."

Yes, this political thriller is the Constitution of the United States of America. It is about a struggle for power, and like most political thrillers, that struggle is established by the authors themselves. The authors recognized that power was indeed a corrupting force. Power vested in a single man or woman could be used to promote domestic tranquility, or just as capriciously could be used to enslave the governed. In this good versus evil genre, the authors knew that no single individual could overcome the temptations of power. Their noble causes of domestic tranquility, common defense, and securing the blessing of liberty required that power not be permitted to consolidate in a single individual. They set up accommodations for continued power struggles and inefficiency and by so doing offered no lodging for tyranny.

Our republic is based upon democratic premises tempered with state's rights. The safeguards of the Constitution are vested in separation of powers not only at the federal level, but between the federal government and the states, with still more rights or liberties reserved directly to the people. The more perfect union is a union of separate states. The Electoral College may appear to be archaic, but it is representative of the distributive nature of power allocation in our system. The Constitution is not a model designed for efficiency. Instead, it is designed for the preservation of representative government.

The greatest fear of the founding fathers was tyranny. That tyranny could come in the form of a popular president unwilling to relinquish his office or an Oliver Cromwell emerging from the legislature. It could also come from the tyranny of mob rule. We would like to think that we have outgrown the need for the protection from the tyranny of mob rule. Before we acclaim ourselves so enlightened, we should first take stock of our emotional nature. The single greatest threat to our nation is our intolerance of its inefficiency and imperfections. Our emotional outcry for efficiency and certainty is an offer to have tyranny as our guest. Before we decide that we have reached the point where we need to reinvent the whole government (yes, the founding fathers even had the sagacity to see that; read the Second Amendment), we should take the time to see why this one works the way it does. If nothing else comes of accepting my invitation to this small investment of time, it should at least move the Constitution to the best seller list. It's a good read.

By Way of England

The following piece addresses the roots of our current system not with regard as to why we have separation of powers, but as to why they are not distinct.

Why Separation of Powers is Not Distinct

If you thought that the last time you would have to hear the term "separation of powers" was in your high school civics class, then the 2000 presidential election certainly spoiled that plan. While the emotional argument in Florida was to count every vote; the real issue at stake was the distribution of power in the entities of our American government. Our system of government sets up three ongoing battles for domestic power. The first revolves around those powers or rights reserved to individuals and those relinquished to various levels of the government. Next, the Constitution divides powers between the federal government and the several states. Finally, power is distributed among the executive, legislative, and judicial branches. This distribution is nearly mirrored at the federal and state levels. It is this last distribution of power which is the source of most conflict.

Tom Spence

Our constitution begins with a noble preamble that enumerates the general scope of our government. Unfortunately, it jumps directly from the purpose to Articles I, II, and III which establish the Legislative, Executive, and Judicial branches without an overall concept of operations. These articles empower and limit but do not generally define how conflicts between or among branches will be resolved. There are some exceptions, specifically enacting legislation, filling vacancies, and impeachment; but as a whole the constitution focuses on three separate entities with little attention paid to boundaries and interaction. This does not diminish the value of what the Founding Fathers provided us. Our Constitution has served us well for 225 years with only infrequent modification, but to truly understand it, we must examine a piece of history that goes beyond our shores.

Our founding fathers were less focused on specific boundaries for each of the branches than they were with providing a lasting foundation that separated them. They dealt first hand with a monarchy that had gradually and begrudgingly divested itself of total sovereignty. The Magna Charta was not a government reinvented from the ground up, but a milestone in power wrestled from a monarch. While the most visible struggle in British Constitutional History is arguably that between the monarch and the parliament; perhaps the most applicable to our

government is that of the Chancellor and his
equitable powers.

About the same time that America was discovered
and colonization began, England faced mounting
problems with its laws. Statutory law was in its
infancy and common law was the preponderance of
the judicial foundation. Unfortunately, common law
did not provide remedies in many situations, most of
them arising out of property arrangements. Such
remedies could only be obtained from the monarch,
or his chief minister--the Chancellor. The Chancellor
was a unique individual. He governed in the king's
council, had some jurisdiction over the common law
courts, and represented the king's conscience. He
could provide extraordinary relief that the courts
could not. He could provide equity. Equity in its
broadest sense denotes the spirit of fairness and
justness. It is justice ascertained by natural reason or
ethical insight but independent of the formulated
body of the law.

The Chancellor was often a bishop, well schooled in
Roman and Canon law. When he found nothing in
the common law, he relied upon his ecclesiastic
training to provide a remedy. In the British power
struggle, the Chancellor was perceived as a threat to
both parliament and the common law courts. While
the Chancellor exercised both legislative and judicial

authority, he was primarily an extension of the monarch—the executive. As the British system evolved, the equitable powers of the Chancellor became less intrusive to the other branches of government through the adoption of equitable principles. Eventually, precedent carried greater weight than individual discretion. This self regulation of the chancery preserved its existence.

When the Constitution of the United States was formulated, equitable power was placed exclusively in the judiciary. What had crossed functional areas in the British system was now reposed in a single branch. What had originally been executive power restrained by the parliament was now wholly vested in one branch of our government. Such a history does not make for a restrained court system. The equitable jurisdiction of the Chancellor allowed him to step across functional boundaries to provide remedies. Even though equity has become much more formalized and governed to a very significant degree by precedent, its roots belie its restriction to a single branch. Equity is the province of the sovereign and resists division.

I advocate judicial restraint and recognize that such a conservative approach will sometimes create selective injustices. That is, the court system will not always be able to provide a remedy. Sometimes, the judiciary must simply wait for the legislature to create a remedy in law. My position is backed by a strict interpretation of the Constitution. Some courts are more active and generally are classified as liberal or activist. They always seek to find a remedy. Their legitimacy is not found in the Constitution but in the history of common law and the equitable jurisdiction of the Chancellor. In a government where power is consolidated in a monarch or dictator, there is no conflict. In a government that has separated basic government functions to prevent tyranny, conflict is inherent in the organization and aggravated by assigning powers not divisible by three to a single branch.

I can offer no alternative without increasing the risk of excessive power consolidated in the executive branch or diluting the power of each branch to impotence. Equitable power is the free safety in football or the rover in softball. It instinctively moves to fill a void in power. It is generally constrained to follow precedent but not restrained by it when new remedies are required. It can serve as the oil that lubricates the wheels of our government or it can grind that same government to a halt to effect an individual remedy. It provides comfort that imperfections will be overcome and anxiety over what those unknown remedies will be. Equity recognizes the divisions of our governmental system but knows no timidity when testing their boundaries. While our founding fathers greatest fear was that a

government of the people would surrender their
plenary power to a power hungry executive; it is the
tool of the monarch's first minister—the equitable
power of the chancellor—that is the wild card in our
system of government. That power is vested in the
judiciary, but by its very nature must venture
elsewhere.

With such a natural disposition to cross functional
boundaries, why would I advocate restraint in a
judiciary vested with equitable powers?   The very
nature of equitable power in 14th century Britain was
nearly its undoing. The equitable power of the
chancellor threatened both parliament and common
law courts, but instead of an overt power struggle,
equity limits were subtly restrained. Such restraint
was not by the parliament or the courts but by the
nature of the equitable power itself. It offered
remedies not elsewhere available and the
Chancellor's court was quickly overwhelmed.
Remedies that supplanted other alternatives available
from the government were self defeating. The most
viable solution was self restraint. Rigidity and
precedent became the rule and new remedies in
equity were reserved for the truly extraordinary case.
Equitable power became formalized and survived the
power struggles of our ancestors. While the
philosophical composition of any court may cause it
to test the boundaries of power; it is equity that
invites a judicial body to boldly journey into the roles
of legislator and executive.   Those exercising such

equitable power know that every such venture comes
with the concomitant that it may be the very event
that topples the delicate balance of separated powers.
Such power must be wielded with exceptional
restraint.

Tom Spence

I pledge allegiance to the flag of the United States of America, and to the republic for which it stands, one nation under God, indivisible, with liberty and justice for all.

Conspiracy Theory

It is the 3rd of November 2010 and I don't know
anyone who voted for Obama in 2008. Seriously, I
don't know a single person who voted for him.
When I think back on it, I don't know anyone that
voted for Bill Clinton in 1992 or 1996 either. I know
some people who voted for him for governor, but not
for president.

Put aside your partisan politics for a moment and
consider this. Most people in the United States do
not remember who they voted for in the last
Presidential Election. I don't remember and I suspect
that you don't either. So you think I'm nuts do you?
Well that may be true, but I'm certain of my facts.

I also have it on good authority that fewer than 600
people voted for Bill Clinton in 1992, and even with
his mandate in 1996, there were fewer than 538 that
voted for him that year. I'm not getting these figures
from some straw poll I conducted in downtown
Burns Flat, America--though that is both the cultural
and political center of this great republic (OK, that
last part is only opinion, but the rest of this article is
fact). Being the only Republican from a family of
Democrats, I often am not taken seriously when I tell
them that I have never met anyone that voted for

Clinton. Still don't believe me? So you want answers? You want the truth? You can't handle the truth. In 1992, only 370 people voted for Clinton. In 1996, only 379 people voted for him, but sure enough that's him in the oval office.

Want to know more? The real election for president didn't occur until December in 1992 and in 1996. We have narrowed it down to 538 people that could have voted for Clinton in 1996--and you thought we conducted elections by secret ballot. Actually, the people that elected our current president even signed their names to their ballot and your government knows who they are. You say that 538 number sounds familiar, but you can't quite place it. It's got nothing to do with the grassy knoll or the number of times that your Microsoft operated computer shuts down each day due to an illegal operation. That's right it's the total number of Senators and Representatives in the United States Congress, but they don't elect the president. In fact, they are not even permitted to vote for the president. So is this coincidence or conspiracy?

Actually, it's neither. It's Article II, Section 1 of the Constitution of the United States of America that provides for the election of a United States President. "Each State shall appoint, in such Manner as the

Legislature thereof may direct, a Number of Electors, equal to the whole Number of Senators and Representatives to which the State may be entitled in the Congress: but no Senator or Representative, or Person holding an Office of Trust or Profit under the United States, shall be appointed an Elector." Yes our president is elected by people we call electors. When you vote in a presidential election, you are voting for electors. We call this group of people the Electoral College. This is a special year in our country's constitutional process. We get to experience both a census and a presidential election. By mid September, when your television is inundated with political commercials and commentaries, you'll probably say "enough with the experience." But with Independence Day still on our minds, this might just be a good time to find a copy of our Constitution and refresh our memories on how we elect a president.

I'll close with a special warning to my Republican brethren. The fox is in the henhouse. Guess who is in charge of counting the votes for the 2000 Presidential Election? You guessed it--Al Gore. That Buddhist Temple stuff is small potatoes compared to this. Speaking of potatoes, wasn't it Dan Quale that was in charge of counting the votes for president in 1992? I knew we should have followed up after that spelling thing...

Tom Spence

This was a piece first published in conjunction with the 2000 election. I occasionally resurrect it during November, on even numbered years, or on days ending with the letter "y" and felt inclined to add a little educational levity to the daunting task that lies ahead of this nation.

The Parable of the Talents

"Again, it will be like a man going on a journey, who called his servants and entrusted his property to them. To one he gave five talents of money, to another two talents, and to another one talent, each according to his ability. Then he went on his journey. The man who had received the five talents went at once and put his money to work and gained five more. So also, the one with the two talents gained two more. But the man who had received the one talent went off, dug a hole in the ground and hid his master's money.

"After a long time the master of those servants returned and settled accounts with them. The man who had received the five talents brought the other five. 'Master,' he said, 'you entrusted me with five talents. See, I have gained five more.'

"His master replied, 'Well done, good and faithful servant! You have been faithful with a few things; I will put you in charge of many things. Come and share your master's happiness!'

"The man with the two talents also came. 'Master,' he said, 'you entrusted me with two talents; see, I have gained two more.'

"His master replied, 'Well done, good and faithful servant! You have been faithful with a few things; I will put you in charge of many things. Come and share your master's happiness!'

"Then the man who had received the one talent came. 'Master,' he said, 'I knew that you are a hard man, harvesting where you have not sown and gathering where you have not scattered seed. So I was afraid and went out and hid your talent in the ground. See, here is what belongs to you.'

"His master replied, 'You wicked, lazy servant! So you knew that I harvest where I have not sown and gather where I have not scattered seed? Well then, you should have put my money on deposit with the bankers, so that when I returned I would have received it back with interest.

"'Take the talent from him and give it to the one who has the ten talents. For everyone who has will be given more, and he will have an abundance. Whoever does not have, even what he has will be taken from him. And throw that worthless servant outside, into the darkness, where there will be weeping and gnashing of teeth.'"

Matthew 25:14-30 NIV

About the Author

Tom Spence is a retired Marine Corps officer. He is an ordained minister in the Cumberland Presbyterian Church. He is husband, father, and grandfather and returned to live in his native Oklahoma in 1999.

As a Marine he served in the First, Second, Third, and Fourth Marine Divisions; as a student and instructor in profession level schools; as a series commander and staff officer at the Marine Corps Recruit Depot, Parris Island, South Carolina; as the Inspector-Instructor on Independent Duty in Des Moines, Iowa; and as a Program Manager in Orlando, Florida. He also served a year with the United Nations as Patrol Base Commander, Sector Operations Officer, and Deputy Commander of the Southern Sector in Iraq and Kuwait (UNIKOM).

He has degrees in political science, biblical studies, theology, and counseling. Beyond his Marine Corps experience, he has been an independent trainer, counselor, and newspaper manager. He is currently the Pastor of the Cumberland Presbyterian Church in Burns Flat, Oklahoma.

His most recent book is *Christianity for Marines*. His other books include *Sea Stories*, *Even the Elect*, *Tough Day at the Plate*, *The Best of **Out of the Box***, and *First Steps Towards Eternity*.

Tom Spence

Tom first began publishing in the late 1980's with a concise article called "MarineSpeak—the modern language of our Corps". That short article in the *Marine Corps Gazette* spoke to the unique language of those called Leatherneck. He later published articles in the *U.S. Naval Proceedings*. They were "Lighten the Load" and "Analog Grunt confronts a Digital World."

Tom publishes hundreds of articles online each year as a freelance author and maintains two blogs: *The Biased Observer* and *Tom's trials, tribulations, and timely thoughts*.

www.thebiasedobserver.com

www.tentalent.blogspot.com

www.theburnsflatnews.com

By Way of Political Affiliation

I am a registered Republican but philosophically closer to the thinking and doctrine of a Libertarian. I am very disappointed in both the Republican and Democrat parties. Both seem to have forgotten that to be of value to the nation, they must serve the people of our nation.

The bitterness, acrimony, vitriol, and unwillingness to do anything other than attempt to gain and maintain power has become the bane of this great republic. That must end.

I frequently communicate this message to elected officials at every level. Some reply, some ignore, and some may take note. I continue to write them.

If someone asks if I am a Republican or Democrat, I ask them what issue they want to discuss. Neither party has a firm value base. Both pander constituencies in hopes of gaining or holding power. We—the American people—have indulged them as they mollify us.

Enough!

It is time to dare greatly once again. If we give our best and still lose our cause, we have dared greatly and are still assured of eternal bliss; but all things considered, I would prefer to dare greatly and succeed greatly.

Therefore we do not lose heart. Though outwardly we are wasting away, yet inwardly we are being renewed day by day. For our light and momentary troubles are achieving for us an eternal glory that far outweighs them all. So we fix our eyes not on what is seen, but on what is unseen, since what is seen is temporary, but what is unseen is eternal.

1 Corinthians 4:16-18

By Way of Faith

I include my spiritual autobiography, which I
published three years ago when I entered the ministry
full time. Since that time, I have been ordained in the
Cumberland Presbyterian Church and serve as Pastor
of the congregation in Burns Flat, Oklahoma.

The Spiritual Autobiography of Tom Spence

May 2008

I begin in the present. I am the stated supply of the
Cumberland Presbyterian Church, Burns Flat,
Oklahoma. One year ago I became the moderator pro
temp[ore] of our session and was instrumental in the
formation of a pastoral search committee. At that
point, I did not envision that I would be the fruit of
that search. That is not to say that I did not expect to
fill the pulpit on a regular basis. I did. I also
expected to reassure the congregation that we would
be just fine, that the head of our church was not the
pastor we didn't have but Christ himself, and that
Christ would still be the head even when we did find
a pastor.

I knew that I was called to be moderator. I knew that
we were a larger church than when I filled the pulpit
between pastors before (2003) and that I would need
more help filling the pulpit. I discovered that we had
grown more than in our numbers. Our ministries had
grown and were still growing. I knew that I needed

to be more involved—more than just filling the pulpit, preparing the bulletin and newsletter, and more than just waiting to see what the search committee would find. I was called to minister to this congregation. Still, I did not expect God to call me to full time ministry. In hindsight, I was in denial—ok, blind—to the fact that God was calling me.

In December 2007, several of the elders, search committee members, and some others from the congregation found our way into the vacant pastor's study. This was following an evening service and this was an impromptu continuation of the fellowship that had begun that evening. Someone asked if I had considered the ministry. The conversation became dominated by that topic. I told everyone that I thought my ministry was to serve the congregation while we searched for another pastor. I did tell them that I would ask God if he was calling me.

I asked. He answered. People that before had not said much to me, told me this was my calling. Instead of the cordial nice sermon remark at the end of the service, peopled hugged me and simply said, go get ordained. People gave me this message in places other than church and many were from other congregations and some were pastors from other denominations. None of them knew of my promise to pray about this.

I would have preferred an email from God, marked important—better yet: URGENT! In fact, after praying, I checked my inbox more frequently than normal. My answer was to come from God's people not my computer. My choice was simple. Kick against the goads and continue to pull my own yoke or accept the one Christ offered. I knew the answer. In a single night, I began my trek to the ministry. I searched the denomination website and was disappointed that there wasn't much there, but I picked a couple email addresses that I thought were appropriate and I also emailed George Estes who had worked with our church in a period of revitalization and whom I kept in the loop on various things going on in Burns Flat. He guided me to Dr. Thomas Dishman Campbell of the Memphis Theological Seminary and to the appropriate committee of the Red River Presbytery. I completed pastor information forms and sent them to the denomination, Red River Presbytery, and made one for our search committee. One of the first things I learned as a Marine officer was that an officer must never be timid and that was the last thing that I was at this point. I had my marching orders and wasn't going to be indecisive. I take comfort in that my Marine Corps background was in perfect harmony here. God did not give us a spirit of timidity.

At the time I gave my package to the search committee, I discovered that they had a candidate that many were excited about. I gave them my packet in a sealed envelope and asked them not to open it if they were actively pursuing a candidate. I knew that I was called to the ministry, but not certain that it would be to my home church congregation. The last thing that I wanted to do was cause any dissent in the committee. At the elders retreat a few days later, I asked for the session's blessing and endorsement to pursue ordination via the program of alternate studies. The session was as excited about my choice as I was.

Some paperwork, interviews, intelligence and psychological evaluations and reports, meetings, and more meetings later brings us to present day: Tom Spence, stated supply at Burns Flat Cumberland Presbyterian Church, endorsed for the PAS by Red River Presbytery, and ready to dive headfirst into this program.

My childhood involved attendance at churches all over the United States; most of them were Disciples of Christ denominations. Sunday School and Vacation Bible School were important events in my life. I was baptized as an adult in the Episcopal Church and married by an Episcopal Navy Chaplain, but most of my adult life was spent in the Presbyterian Church with a few ventures into Baptist congregations. I had never heard of the Cumberland Presbyterian Church until I moved to Burns Flat in 1999. The first service I attended told me that this would be our church home. Before joining, I invited the Pastor to the house and we discussed several things. I wanted to make sure of the central beliefs of this denomination and to make sure it wasn't some off the wall sect. Jim Fisk was the pastor at the time and he gave me a one minute history of the denomination and answered my questions. He was interested in how a Marine officer had reconciled being a professional combatant and a Christian as his son was currently serving in the Army.

A significant part of my adult life was as a U.S. Marine Corps officer. I see no dichotomy between battle and serving God. God has called many to battle. While my time in a combat zone was only one year out of twenty; preparing for battle on a daily basis has helped me in my current spiritual journey. I truly enjoyed my time in the Marine Corps. Among other things, I learned to be a life-long learner in the Corps. To learn and master new skills every year is still a passion of mine. To teach, train, mentor, and see the fruits of your efforts in young men and women is an experience that few enjoy to the extent I experienced as a Marine. I believe that my time in the Corps was a blessing from God.

I have no Road to Damascus experience. I was taught, I believed, and I have grown in my faith. That's not to say I have not had trials. I have and for the most part they have strengthened me. Those that have not are because I struggled against what God wanted me to do. Surrender is a tough word for a Marine to pronounce, but I learned when I surrendered all to Christ, He gave me victory.

All in my family are saved. Sharman, my wife, and I both love our church family. She is an elementary teacher and that is also her ministry. Burns Flat is a town with a large transient population. Many children she teaches have parents in prison, using drugs in their presence, or who are absent from their lives. Much of the love that these children receive comes from Sharman in the classroom. We cannot go anywhere in southwest Oklahoma without getting hugged by knee-high people. I have also become an expert shopper of crayons, pencils, and folders. If K-Mart is having a blue light special on school supplies during my time at Bethel College, I will need a 1-hour excused absence to go buy a cubic meter of crayons.

Both my children, Heather and Christopher, are out of the house and doing their best to make their own way in the world. I have no grandchildren yet, but cherish the fact that God through his grace has better prepared me for that role now that I know Him better. My body is 52 years old and I put it through some pounding during my time in the Corps; but, my excitement to pursue fulltime ministry is as intense as any I have experienced. I get out of bed in the morning ready to see what God wants me to do today!

Semper Fidelis!

Tom Spence

Since I originally published this, I have become a grandfather, completed by program of study from Memphis Theological Seminary to include the summer sessions at Bethel College (now Bethel University), been examined, licensed, examined again, ordained, and installed as Pastor. In short, the first part of the journey that I have been called to is complete. The best part—living the calling for which I have been set apart—is surely ahead of me.

Semper Fidelis and **Amen**!

Tom Spence

Old Corps

Back in the Old Corps, we had a saying. If you were accused of being a Marine, would there be enough evidence to convict you. I close this brief treatise with similar challenges.

If you were accused of being a patriot, would there be enough evidence to convict you?

If you were accused of being a Christian, would there be enough evidence to convict you?

If you were accused to leaving this nation and this world a better place than when you arrived in it, would there be enough evidence to convict you?